Look Out!

Story by Jenny Giles

Illustrations by Rachel Tonkin

Kylie and Zoe came out
of their classroom.

They looked at all the children
who were playing outside.

"I want to go and play
by the trees," said Zoe.
"But we can't."

"No," said Kylie.
"When we go past the wall,
  some big girls jump out at us."

"And I always get scared," said Zoe.
"Let's just stay here and play."

4

"I can't see the girls today,"
  said Kylie.
"We could try and get past the wall."

"But they will be hiding behind it
  and waiting for us," said Zoe.
"When we get there,
  they will jump out at us."

"No they won't," said Kylie.
"They are not always there."

Zoe and Kylie
walked slowly over to the wall.
Then they saw one of the girls
looking around it.

Kylie and Zoe stopped.

The big girls **were** hiding
behind the wall.

"Let's go back to our room,"
said Zoe.

Just then, Miss Bell
came walking by.

As she got to the end of the wall,
the big girls jumped out.
What a surprise they got
when they saw a teacher!

Miss Bell got a surprise, too.
She was very angry
with the big girls.
"Come here, all of you!" she said.
"That was a very silly thing to do.
You could have hurt someone!"

The girls looked at Miss Bell.
"Sorry!" they said.

But Miss Bell was still angry.
"Now stay away from here!" she said.
"I don't want to tell you again!
You must **never** jump out like that!"

Kylie and Zoe started to laugh.
"The big girls looked so funny
when they saw Miss Bell,"
said Kylie.

"Yes," said Zoe.
"And now they will **never**
jump out at us again."